Dedication

For Eva; you are always so thoughtful and kind to others. Never lose that.

Copyright

© Copyright 2025 Deb Pickering. All Rights Reserved.
It is illegal to reproduce, duplicate or transmit any part of this document in either electronic means or printed format. Recording of this publication is strictly prohibited.

Carrot Cake for my Daddy!

Eva loves to bake when she goes to her nana's house but for a long time, when asked what she wanted to bake, she would immediately reply, "Carrot cake for my daddy, 'coz that's his favourite cake!"

She made it so often, that she could tell her nana what ingredients were needed – without even looking at a recipe! And now, when her grandparents see carrot cake of any kind, they call it, 'carrot cake for my daddy'!

"Nana, please can we bake today?"
"Of course! What shall we make?"

"Carrot cake for my daddy 'coz that's his favourite cake.

And can we make a podcast, that I can send to Mum?
Then later on today, she can see what we have done!"

Nana set up her mobile, and Eva pressed record.
"Hi, my name is Eva, and if you're feeling bored,

You've come into the right place, 'coz we're going to have some fun.
We're making carrot cake today, that's yummy when it's done.

You first go to your nana's, and ask if you can bake.
And then add the ingredients, to your bowl, to make your cake.

You'll need flour, eggs and sugar and of course margarine,

But also carrots, raisins, nutmeg and tangerine.

You mix them all together, then when the mixing's done:
Put them into the oven, in a cake tin, or as buns.

When they are cool you ice them, then give them to your dad.

And they will be the 'most amazing cakes he's ever had!'"

Carrot Cake Recipe

Ingredients
For the cake:

- 265g self-raising flour
- 225g margarine (or olive oil can be used instead)
- 4 large eggs
- 265g muscovado sugar
- 265g carrots, grated
- 200g sultanas
- 2½ tsp ground cinnamon
- ½ fresh nutmeg, grated
- 1 orange, zest only (or zest of 3 tangerines)

For the icing:

- 100g butter, softened
- 300g icing sugar
- 100g soft cheese (e.g., cream cheese)

Method

1. Preheat the oven to 180°C (Gas Mark 4).
2. Prepare your tins: Grease two 20cm cake tins or line muffin tins with cupcake papers.
3. In a large bowl, mix all the dry ingredients: flour, sugar, cinnamon, nutmeg, and sultanas.
4. In a separate bowl, combine the wet ingredients: margarine (or oil), eggs, carrots, and orange zest.
5. Add the wet ingredients to the dry ingredients and mix well until fully combined.
6. Divide the mixture evenly between your prepared tins or cupcake cases.
7. Bake:

                     For cake tins: 25–30 minutes
                     For cupcakes: 15–20 minutes

Check with a skewer—if it comes out clean, the cake is ready.
8. Cool in tins before turning out onto a wire rack.

To make the icing:
1. Beat the butter and icing sugar together until smooth.
2. Add half the soft cheese and mix gently.
3. Once incorporated, add the remaining cheese and mix until just combined.
Tip: Avoid overmixing the cheese to prevent the icing from splitting.

Can you point to each of the ingredients that are in Eva's Carrot cake?

self-raising flour
eggs
muscovado sugar
carrots
sultanas
cinnamon
whole nutmeg
orange (or tangerines)
butter,
icing sugar

About the Author

Deb Pickering is a nana of 3 gorgeous grandchildren, who lives in York with her husband. She loves being an active part of the children's lives and says, "They are an absolute inspiration, and better still, they make me laugh, which keeps me young!"

www.ingramcontent.com/pod-product-compliance
Lightning Source LLC
Chambersburg PA
CBHW041120070526
44584CB00002B/225